INDEPENDENCE
DAY

Peachtree

Joanna Ponto

Enslow Publishing
101 W. 23rd Street
Suite 240
New York, NY 10011
USA
enslow.com

Published in 2016 by Enslow Publishing, LLC.
101 W. 23rd Street, Suite 240, New York, NY 10011

Library of Congress Cataloging-in-Publication Data
Ponto, Joanna, author.
 Independence Day / Joanna Ponto.
    pages cm— (the story of our holidays)
 Includes bibliographical references and index.
 Audience: Grade 4 to 6.
 ISBN 978-0-7660-7459-0 (library binding)
 ISBN 978-0-7660-7471-2 (pbk.)
 ISBN 978-0-7660-7465-1 (6 pack)
 1. Fourth of July—Juvenile literature. 2. Fourth of July celebrations—Juvenile literature. I. Title.
 E286.A158 2016
 394.2634—dc23
                          2015032643

Printed in the United States of America

To Our Readers: We have done our best to make sure all website addresses in this book were active and appropriate when we went to press. However, the author and the publisher have no control over and assume no liability for the material available on those websites or on any websites they may link to. Any comments or suggestions can be sent by e-mail to customerservice@enslow.com.

Portions of this book originally appeared in the book *Independence Day: Birthday of the United States.*

Photos Credits: Cover, p. 1 Arina P Habich/Shutterstock.com; p. 4 iStock.com/Steve Debenport; p. 6 Library of Congress, Prints and Photographs Division; p. 8 I. Pilon/Shutterstock.com; p. 12 © North Wind Picture Archives; p. 14 redswept/Shutterstock.com; p. 18 Linda Davidson/The Washington Post/Getty Images; p. 21 Sabrina Cercelovic/Shutterstock.com; p. 23 SuperStock/SuperStock; p. 24 Kevin M. Kerfoot/Shutterstock.com; p. 26 Christian Petersen/Getty Images; p. 31 Karen Huang; p. 32 Susan Leggett/Shutterstock.com.

Contents

Americans enjoy celebrating their nation's independence.

Chapter 1

Happy Birthday, America!

No matter where you look, there are celebrations. Fireworks! Picnics! Parades! Red, white, and blue streamers are everywhere. Hot dogs cook on the grill. Children wave small flags. People across America are celebrating. It must be July 4, Independence Day.

Celebrating Our Country

Everyone has a birthday, and so does America. The United States of America was born on July 4, 1776. Before that,

Up in the Sky! Fireworks!

Fireworks are a fun and exciting way to celebrate America's birthday. They help us to remember the fight that took place for our independence.

The signing of the Declaration of Independence was the birth of a new nation—the United States of America.

the king of England ruled. On July 4, Americans declared their independence. The United States would become a new nation with its own laws, leaders, and flag.

In 1776, people celebrated their independence from England. Today, Americans still remember their nation's birthday. Every July 4, they celebrate.

Chapter 2

Independence!

When America started out, it was not made up of fifty states. There were just thirteen colonies. These colonies were settlements that belonged to England. They were scattered along the East Coast of North America.

Finding Freedom

Most of the people in the American colonies were born in England. They came to the colonies hoping for a better life. Some hoped to find freedom in this new land. But many of the colonists did not think they had found that freedom.

King George III ruled England. He also ruled the American colonies. The king asked a lot of the colonists. England was a

In 1776, there were thirteen states that made up the United States of America.

powerful country. It had many soldiers, weapons, and armed ships.

But it took a great deal of money for England to stay that powerful.

The thirteen American colonies created businesses and farmed the

land to make money for England.

8

Taxes: They Weren't Fair

England's soldiers protected the American colonies, so England's king felt that taxes should be paid to him for this protection. A tax is money from the sale of things such as molasses, sugar, stamps, or tea. The colonists believed they were not being taken care of by the king and did not want to pay the taxes. The king sent soldiers to the American colonies to make sure that the taxes were paid. The colonists had to provide places to stay and food for the soldiers.

The colonists decided the king of England was unfair, so they took action. In 1774, a leader from each of the American colonies met in Philadelphia, Pennsylvania. This meeting became known as the Continental Congress. The leaders of the colonies talked about the problems they shared. They knew the people wanted things to change even if it meant fighting for those changes.

War!

By 1775, fighting broke out between the king's soldiers and the American colonists. The king's troops had better weapons and more training, but the colonists were fighting for their freedom. They also knew their land well.

The Continental Congress met again in May 1775. This time the leaders of the colonies talked about their goals and hopes. They argued about what was best for the colonies.

At last, they decided to break away from England's rule. The colonies would become a new, independent nation. That new nation would be known as the United States of America.

Declaration of Independence

Thomas Jefferson, a leader from the Virginia colony, was at the Second Continental Congress. The other leaders asked him to write down their ideas. Jefferson knew what the colonists were thinking and feeling. Now he had to write it all down. This was not easy work. Those words would become the plan for a new nation, and those words would make history.

Jefferson worked on the statement from June 11 to June 28. Then he showed it to the other leaders at the Second Continental Congress. They called the statement the Declaration of Independence. The leaders finally agreed on its exact wording on

July 4, 1776. This is why July 4, the birthday of the United States, is also called Independence Day.

The First Celebration

In Philadelphia, Pennsylvania, people gathered in the streets. They heard the Declaration of Independence read. They cheered and hugged each other as bells rang and bands played.

Colonists in other places celebrated, too. There were parades, and cannons and muskets were fired. There were speeches and special dinners. People celebrated their new nation.

In New York, the colonists were busy. They tore down a statue of King George III. But they did not want to waste any of the metal

July 8, 1776

Every year on July 4 in the United States of America, we celebrate our independence. But the first Independence Day was celebrated on July 8, 1776. Long ago, in the days before telephones and television, news traveled slowly by horseback or ship. It took many days for copies of the Declaration of Independence to reach all thirteen American colonies.

Colonists were glad to be free of British rule.

from the statue. They needed bullets to fight the British soldiers. So they used the metal from the statue to make the bullets.

The colonists needed many bullets. Their struggle for freedom was far from over. They fought King George and his soldiers for seven more years in what is known as the Revolutionary War, or the American Revolution. In 1783, they finally won the war. Now they were no longer colonists. Instead, they were free citizens of the United States of America.

Chapter 3

Marching, Munchies, and More

No celebration is like an Independence Day celebration. They are noisy, colorful, and fun. There are lots of different ways to enjoy July 4, some dating back to the time of the American colonists.

Flash, Crash, Boom!

There have always been fireworks on July 4, but they were not always like what we have today. Early fireworks were simple and often seen near harbors. Military ships fired off rockets over the water.

Firework displays are a common way for communities to celebrate Independence Day.

The rockets lit up the sky, but they cost a lot of money. The colonists were still fighting King George, and they did not have extra money. So they brightened the holiday by putting candles in every window.

Today, fireworks are loud and flashy. They remind us of the colonists firing cannons. Some fireworks look like sparkling pinwheels, and others look like streamers. Still others seem like a shower of stars. Fireworks come in just about every color imaginable.

Some firework displays are shown on the ground. Often these are shaped like objects or animals. One favorite is a red, white, and blue American flag. Another is a bald eagle. Both of these things are symbols of the United States. A symbol is something that stands for something else. When people see bald eagles and American flags, they think of the United States.

There are also other ways to light up Independence Day. Some larger cities have skyline celebrations. The tops of the tallest buildings are lit in red, white, and blue. The Empire State Building in New York City is one. The result is an all-American skyline.

The Importance of Parades

Parades are an important part of Independence Day. In colonial times, soldiers marched. As time passed, things changed. Fire trucks and police departments became part of the parade.

Independence Day parades have grown larger than they used to be. Soldiers from America's past wars often march. Groups of Boy or Girl Scouts may take part along with high school marching bands.

Many parades have red, white, and blue floats of patriotic scenes. The people on them may dress in costumes and toss pieces of candy into the crowds of people watching. Community groups and elected officials, such as the mayor, smile and wave to everyone.

The people watching the parade are also part of the fun. People line the streets, wave small American flags, and cheer for the marchers.

Washington, DC, the nation's capital, has an especially large parade. Hundreds of thousands of people come to see it. Bands from all over the country take part.

The Independence Day parade in Aptos, California, is unusual. It is the world's shortest parade because it is only three blocks long.

However, it takes more than two hours to see because it has so many marchers and floats.

Aptos is a fairly small town. Some say that about half the people in town march in the parade. The rest of the people watch.

Mouth-Watering Munchies

Food has always been an important part of celebrating Independence Day. It probably would not be as much fun without the food. In colonial times special dinners were served. The best dishes and silverware were used.

By the 1800s, things began to change. Independence Day celebrations were more relaxed. Sometimes people who were running for an elected office had big feasts. This was a good way to meet the voters.

A "Horrible" Parade

There is a special parade for children in Marblehead, Massachusetts. It is called the Fourth of July Horribles Parade. It was created to help children pass the long day waiting for the fireworks to start. Hundreds of young people come to the parade wearing funny or unusual costumes.

Uncle Sam is a common sight at Independence Day parades.

Picnics became popular. Families packed baskets and headed to parks. Lots of other families gathered. Some played volleyball and baseball. People also liked to pitch horseshoes, and there was music. If the park had a lake, people might swim. Sometimes they went rowing in boats.

One of the largest Fourth of July picnics was in Ontario, California, in 1956. It was known as the All-States Picnic, and people came from all over America. More than one hundred thousand people came.

Americans still enjoy picnics on the Fourth of July. Many people grill hot dogs and hamburgers. They may also have baked beans, potato salad, and corn on the cob. These foods are all Fourth of July favorites.

Not everyone goes to a park to celebrate. Often friends and family get together in their backyards. People in cities might grill on their balconies and terraces.

There are some tasty Independence Day desserts, too. Some people like a cool slice of watermelon. Others prefer a red, white, and blue treat. Children often like to cool off with frozen desserts like ice cream or sundaes. See page 20 for a colorful and tasty sundae recipe. On Independence Day, the red, white, and blue striped ones seem to taste best.

Independence Day Ice Cream Sundae*

Red, white, and blue desserts are perfect for an Independence Day celebration. You don't have to stick to these exact ingredients. Have fun using your favorite red, white, and blue fruits and treats.

You will need the following supplies:

- a plastic knife*
- strawberries
- a red or blue plastic dish for the ice cream
- a spoon
- vanilla ice cream
- mini marshmallows
- blueberries
- red and blue candy-covered chocolate pieces
- a maraschino cherry

Directions:

1. With the help of an adult, carefully cut the strawberries in half with the plastic knife.
2. Place the strawberry halves in the plastic dish and stand them on their sides.
3. Use the spoon to place one scoop of vanilla ice cream in the center of the dish.
4. Sprinkle mini marshmallows over the ice cream.
5. Sprinkle blueberries and the pieces of chocolate over the ice cream.
6. Put the cherry on top. Enjoy your cool Fourth of July treat!

* Adult supervision required.

Chapter 4

One Hundredth and Two Hundredth Birthdays

No matter where it's celebrated, Independence Day is always a great time. Two Independence Days, however, are famous.

One Hundred

One was our country's centennial, or one hundredth, birthday. It took place in 1876. The biggest celebration was in Philadelphia, Pennsylvania. The city had a huge fair called the International Exposition. People from many countries from all over the world came to help Americans celebrate.

That Independence Day, Americans also had another special event. The public was shown a new painting of a battlefield

The Spirit of '76

This painting is called *The Spirit of '76*. It shows three men leading American soldiers into battle. Many people feel it shows the courage of America's soldiers.

scene from the American Revolution. The artist was Archibald Willard, an American from Bedford, Ohio. Willard named the painting *The Spirit of '76*. The '76 stands for the year 1776, when America declared its independence from England. The painting hung in Memorial Hall in Philadelphia, Pennsylvania. Many people felt it showed the courage of our soldiers. Today the painting is famous. It hangs in Abbot Hall in Marblehead, Massachusetts.

Two Hundred

Our country's two hundredth birthday was even more spectacular. This birthday was known as the bicentennial, and there were many activities. People in Boston made a giant Independence Day pancake that measured seventy-six inches—more than six feet—across. They also baked a huge cake that weighed sixty-nine thousand pounds. In Sheboygan, Wisconsin, people celebrated by participating in sports and games. They tossed 1,776 Frisbees into the air.

Washington, DC, had the country's largest fireworks display. It cost nearly a quarter of a million dollars. New York City hosted Operation Sail, where many tall ships sailed into New York harbor. More than two hundred smaller ships did the same thing. Thousands of people came to watch. There were also many other celebrations throughout the United States. By the end of the day, it was clear that the United States had had a wonderful two hundredth birthday.

This flag was designed and flown for the nation's two hundredth birthday.

Chapter 5

Celebrations All Over America

Everyone enjoys having lots of fun. People are always thinking of new and exciting ways to celebrate. This is especially true for Americans on Independence Day. Some towns have holiday concerts, while others have talent shows. There are also beauty contests.

Patriotic Parties

Many places put on patriotic skits or shows. Battle scenes from the Revolutionary War may be acted out. Children can enjoy pony rides, and families may go up in hot air balloons.

Imagine what it would be like to celebrate the Fourth of July with the United States Marines. This is exactly what some people in Albany, Georgia, have done since 1994. The public is invited to attend a celebration hosted by the United States Marine Corps. There are country music concerts, carnival rides, fireworks, and much more. The idea behind the day is simple. The Marines believe we should "celebrate Independence Day with those who keep you independent."

Independence Day rodeos are a common way for communities to celebrate.

Independence Day in Prescott, Arizona, has a Western theme. The town has a weekend celebration called Frontier Days. The event includes a rodeo, bronco riders, and cowboys who come from near and far to compete and watch the events.

Philadelphia, Pennsylvania, always has great Fourth of July celebrations. After all, the Declaration of Independence was signed there. The last Independence Day in the twentieth century was on

July 4, 1999. It was remembered in Philadelphia in a special way. The Photo of the Century was taken in front of Independence Hall. The photograph shows one hundred Americans of all different ages who were born on July 4. Each person was born in a different year from 1900 to 1999. People from all fifty states were in the photo.

You Have the Right to . . . Have Fun!

The Independence Day celebration in Seward, Nebraska, is unusual. The sheriff starts the fun on July 3. He stops a car that is traveling along Interstate 80, but it is not just any car. He always picks a car with out-of-state license plates that has a family inside.

A Sky-High Good Time

For some people, Independence Day is extra special. On this day, some people go up in hot air balloons.

The sheriff does not arrest these people. Instead, he gives them a chance to have a great Fourth of July. The family is invited to spend the night at a local motel free of charge. The next day, they celebrate Independence Day with the town. The guest family can march in the parade and enjoy a pancake breakfast.

All-American Activities

People in the town of George in the state of Washington celebrate in a big way. They make a huge cherry pie that is eight feet wide and eleven feet high. It is made with half a ton of fruit, and pieces of the pie are given out for free. Afterward, there is another show when the fire department hoses down the empty pie pan.

Minturn, Colorado, has an all-day block party. There are pie and hot dog eating contests. Everyone also enjoys the dog show and the carnival. There is plenty of food for everyone.

The Fourth of July can also be fun for people who live near lakes and rivers. Many people like to spend the holiday on or near the water. This is exactly what happens every Independence Day on Lake Mohawk in New Jersey. People swim and water ski during the day. When it gets dark, they can watch the fireworks from their boats.

Americans may celebrate Independence Day in different ways, but they are all celebrating the same thing. Every year, on July 4, we honor the birth of our nation. Our country stands for freedom, and there can never be too many ways to celebrate that.

Independence Day Craft

M ake a safe sparkler to bring to a parade and wave around.

Here are the supplies you will need:

Twelve 1-inch-wide strips of ribbon— four red, four white, four blue

Newspaper

Glue

Glitter

A blue marker or crayon

The cardboard tube from an empty roll of toilet paper.

A small box of star stickers (silver ones look best, but any color will do)

Directions:

1. Separate the ribbon strips by color and lay them flat on the newspaper. Glue glitter onto one side of each ribbon.

2. When the glue is dry and the glitter is sticking, turn each ribbon over and glue glitter on the other side. Let the glue dry.

3. With the blue marker or crayon, color the cardboard tube.

4. Decorate the tube with the star stickers.

5. Apply glue to one end of each ribbon. Glue the ends of the ribbons to the inside of the cardboard tube. Let the glue dry.

6. Have some fun with your sparkler!

Make a Glitter Sparkler

*Safety Note: Be sure to ask for help from an adult, if needed, to complete this project.

Glossary

century—One hundred years.

colonist—A person who lives in a colony.

colony—A settlement. There were thirteen English colonies before the United States became a nation.

exposition—A large fair or event attended by many people.

historic—Having to do with the past.

musket—A large firearm. Muskets were used as weapons in colonial times.

patriotic—Showing love and loyal support for one's country.

spectacular—Something that is unusually good or outstanding.

tax—Money from the sale of things such as molasses, sugar, stamps, or tea.

territory—A region or area of land.

Some Americans enjoy watersports, like water-skiing, on the Fourth of July.

Learn More

Books

DeRubertis, Barbara. *Let's Celebrate Independence Day* (Holidays & Heroes). New York: The Kane Press, 2016.

Donaghey, Reese. *The History of Independence Day* (What You Didn't Know About History). New York: Gareth Stevens, 2015.

Owen, Ruth. *Independence Day Origami* (Holiday Origami). New York: PowerKids Press, 2012.

Websites

Fourth of July Facts

kidskonnect.com/holidays-seasons/fourth-july

Check out facts about the Fourth of July.

Happy Birthday America

usacitylink.com/usa

Learn facts, songs, and more related to the Fourth of July.

Happy Fourth of July!

timeforkids.com/news/happy-fourth-july/41766

Facts and quizzes teach you about Independence Day.

Index